my sweet unconditional

ariel robello

Tia Chucha Press
Los Angeles

ACKNOWLEDGMENTS

With all honor and respect to the Creator/a whose guidance has made the journey possible.
I ask your help for the road ahead.

With mil gracias to my mother for never giving up on me.

With love for my father who taught me to look at the world with a painter's eye.

With a song for my family on the other side, in my heart there are no lines between us.

With humble affection for the writing communities of The World Stage, PEN West, Los Angeles, San Diego, San Francisco, New York and Washington DC—you have all inspired me to step out of my shell and brave the work everyday.

With props to my students for their support, your poems are the glue in my life.

With much respect for Luis and Tia Chucha Press for keeping your word and seeing that my words found their way to these pages, I look forward to the work ahead.

With love to my friends whose enduring belief and unconditional love allowed me to see the dream through.

ISBN 1-882688-29-5

Book design: Jane Brunette
Cover illustration: Serina Koester, Ariel Robello and Rhea Vedro
Back cover photo: Justin M. Jobst

PUBLISHED BY:
Tía Chucha Press
PO Box 328
San Fernando CA 91341

DISTRIBUTED BY:
Northwestern University Press
Chicago Distribution Center
11030 South Langley Avenue
Chicago IL 60628

Tía Chucha Press is supported by the National Endowment for the Arts and operating funds from Tía Chucha's Centro Cultural – www.tiachucha.com.

TABLE OF CONTENTS

LA GATA

I drank to drown my pain,
but the damned pain learned how to swim,
and now I'm overwhelmed
by this decent and good behavior.

FRIDA KAHLO

ANGELES ASADA

They are burning the bodies tonight.

The crematorium on 8th Street don't hide its stench
from the staggered silhouettes of drunken men
who spend every cent on brown-bagged bottles of hope
tonight the barrio hums *De Colores* and low rider tunes
as people cope with fragrant asada of human flesh
shielded in hibiscus pink and Acapulco blue homes
these nights a test for spirits stuck in crude oil of fronteralands.

Memo squashes black ants with his bare feet
under an orange moon I trace my name in the stars
we own this hillside view
where ghettos are fallen galaxies
and poverty she is down right pretty tonight.

You promised we would live free... "mas alla de la razon"
and that "all would be alright"
only here, there is no magic carpet ride
no up and away
just Memo blowing *El Rey* on a blade of dry grass
and a German shepherd's ears tuned to renegade radio station.

Tune out Miranda   tune in revolution   baby

Memo whispers wet Spanglish in my ear
but all I hear is the woman next door praying between sobs
hoping God will subdue her old man's temper
Memo can't hear what wars he's survived
her screams like shrapnel won't penetrate his thick skin
his hand weaves its way between my thighs
and Mr. DJ say *all is all right*   *yeah*   *all is all right*
only here, there is no magic carpet ride
no up and away
just a tagging crew playing quarters
on the unmarked tomb of a forgotten soldier.

Hungry for coconut juice and cool ripe melon
we slow dance into K-LOVE late night forgiveness
then make love on an old mattress
Memo strung out on sky, me strung out on fear
cause that's how we collect strikes
at the intersection where first generation and ancient meet
where corn vendors and chrome saddle cement
where shopping carts and homeboys come home bent
and every one counts angels making their way through the sky.

Cause here, there is no magic carpet ride
no up and away for the living
no shiny pennies
early refunds
or middle age
from smoke stack to lung
hope steams crooked, sweet tipped and tender
as the bodies burn I let myself surrender
to the only thing that never changes
my love for the boy who plays Mariachi on the wings of daisies.

SUS CONSEJOS

Mama said, "Latin loves don't last long."
(stick to your own kind)
she knows how hard
to sleep so good
too late for her
for me he's gone
under my skin another splinter
under my sheet another crumb.

Papa said, "You want a doctor, someone to take care of you."
(stick to your own kind)
he knows how hard to slap
brown on white won't stick
he knew he'd quit
he knew love lies
in my bed
under my skin
sticking not stuck.

"Stick to your own kind, m'ija."
I know to last
I must deny love of self
to find my kind
I know they said they know what's best
but still I make my love in mud.

HOME

where I'm from real people eat tacos at 4 a.m.
drunk and high they enjoy freedom of D

                                    R
                                        O
                                          P top

low
low
low riders
with neon bass and no where
no where to go
real people lie steal and smoke their lives away
angry and undereducated
real people need drama and day jobs
to occupy voids between hangovers
and month late car payments

confined to waiting rooms
real people stare down
real people under florescent lights
they print their names at the X with a lucky pen
for a chance at free checking and chest exams

with security cameras watching
real people dance with mannequins
after closing real people sweat
under heat lamps their bodies melding
into one seamless happy ending

once a flaming rabbit's foot
fell through the black top
of my real world
the roof
the roof
the roof is on fire
it was the first time

i.   la gata loca
saw a hole to the other side
where the best years of real life
were worth more than a slow dance with number 33
on the all star team

for me the thunder of my feet
pounding what's real into molehills behind me
is as loud as the night I decided to hunt the wildebeest of more

LET ME RIDE

let me ride in the lover's car
where I am Iztaccihuatl on his lap
white volcano before war
bass rumbling below us
warnings from fault lines undecided
which side we'll choose

it takes an hour to go one mile down the Strip
that is three lights
his fingers tapping Morse code inside
the lover's car where bras are left like surrender flags
and perfect bald heads grow wet with cinnamon kisses

I want to be the Aztec calendar girl
mounted between his shrine to la Virgin and Teena Marie
hickeys framing my charm necklace
laughing at bullhorn warnings
from policemen too afraid to talk shit to our faces

it is before curfew, graduation and Uncle Sam's nagging plea
to be all you can be on this night
you must ride, 15 mph, detailed and louder than your neighbor
you must know which hand signs peace and which will launch wanton action
you must bite down hard on your urge to outrun
every other hard shell in the race

let me ride backseat immune to stop signs
pilfering seconds before life calls
before we become hazy interpretations of what they'd have us be
before laptops and DSL, Afghanistan and dress pants
before credit checks, regrets, training camps, freshman politics, rudimentary
skills we'll need to survive after this night
steady driver, we're making time stand still back here
steady, we're undressing worm holes back here
steady, we ain't ready to go home just yet

TUFF MEDICINE

Oye nena!
this poem is tuff medicine
made up of 2 parts naked storm
3 part mercenary men
4 part petalpusher
1 part oxygen

I dub dub dare ya
become electric buttafly
come on sour angel stop frontin
you holdin up traffic in your veins
you slumlordin your soul

precious peahen penned into your "Stories"
dying to dig up roots of someone else's pain
no one won here
worse yet
no one ever will

dig this vision
one twelve foot neon WIC sign
it took six men to climb the pole
black birds with fat bellies
to align the holes
just right   all day   all night
you keep your Venus intact
cry anti-freeze
when he's late to your 3 a.m. dream
the one when you ride Coney Island's *Earthquake*
10 times in a row
shaken from outside-in
you find a way to forgive

from top twin tenement towers
Big Boi screams   *Perdoname!*
into a universal megaphone
they come quick
take him in for inciting a riot

it takes life to live here
steady hands to hold the rails

child I dub dub dare ya
play the panic down
calm your tracks with cocoa butta
and become sweet face of nowhere

THE NIGHT THE DJ SAVED MY LIFE

for New York after hours

his eyes split the dance floor

his lips split the groove of my smile
his vinyl smooth caress took one breast and fed an island nation
between the ebb and his tongue
a spinning table of reasons
why not
come
undone

we stood erect
pulsing time into timba
laughter then dip into back board marimba
equal shots of mambo & lime
his finger epidermal needles
retracting inhibition from my spine
in   slow   slide   scratch
we held our breath exhaled and came in time

sigh   all that's left of the DJ that saved my life
is a mixed tape and over 18 glowing under black light

RAVE POLITICS

you can look but don't touch the butterflies
an angel is a death trap with wings
space aliens are open to solicitations
white pills will make your skin peel off
the blue ones will put it back on
don't take a first date
if your friends multiply before your eyes
take off the glasses
if they grow another head
gently push it back in
a bad dancer is probably a Narc
not everybabydoe is looking at you
two is boring
three or more is showbiz
when you take off in the red balloon don't look down
when you land   don't look up
fire-breathing dragons will deflate
when driving into nowhere gas up and buy tic tacs
to   t r a i l   behind you
if glass shards spin all around
pretend they're sugar plum fairies
but whatever you do never
no never stop dancing

RAPPER'S DELIGHT

hello of cleavage
cinch of stretch denim
poison sprayed cross your ass & chest

against the wall you a Malaysian carving
invisible basket of dreams balanced on your head
your curves calling men to reel you in

the back seat a sweat lodge
frost of nights you called home from pay phone
half whimper half spit
left because you wouldn't —
no couldn't — why do you resist?

and how they scorned your rebellion
threw the mic in your face
back stage a race to the after party
where they took turns inside you
while you'd wait for your Savior to come

in hotel lobby they'd rub reason and meter
in your ears a buzz of something you had to say
burning behind your teeth a wad of gum
clicking tongue of paces

you blew on the dice
won a shadow deal behind emcee of the week
graduate of street games (invented and real)
emory board routine on acrylic nails
filing holes in your head heart womb
where poem or love or baby might have grown
had you'd owned your free will

against the wall you look angelic
wide-eyed with magnetic pull of spotlights
high of his hand moving up your thigh

see girl, a rapper's delight always delivers sunshine
until she's sent home at sunrise black-eyed and broken

THE RUNWAY

Hailey's comet tears down La Cienega Blvd.
splitting the car wash
open like a hooker's thighs

blisters rise on Randy's giant doughnut
sweet confections and garbage men
scramble for their lives

the unfortunate driver
stuck at the eternal red light
glass cut palms
a lifetime of gripping the wheel
too tight

the misunderstood sky
a field of bloody salutations
waving hello

goodbye.

IN YOUR FACE LOVE

trapped in cul-de-sacs and Denny's bathrooms
the loyal are tested to see how much split your bottom lip can take
on the other side of love is a brown boy
who never meant to hurt you

asleep in alleys and on stained sheets at Motel 6
the one between Pal's Happy Liquor and Emerald City Express
with noodles and malt beer to fill the dying beast
in your face love forgets which hand struck first
who did what when and why even friends don't question no more

spider web in the corner
prey tired and sufficiently numb
the hourglass on your neck
accessory to a crime you'll claim you like it rough
each welt proof enough
you're no body 'til somebody loves you

in your face love like the first 18 days in Vietnam
a lifetime of seizures
virgin nostrils in a field of rusty poppies
like winter in Belgrade and summer in Harlem
in your face love's a lightening rod in the grip of an iron man
a covenant of Sunday slow jams
a Rolls Royce in quick sand
in your face love is La Motta vs. Sugar Ray 1951
in the 13th round saying I never went down
no, for this love I stood standing

CARTA PERSONAL

Abuelita's hands wake me
soft as masa they tell of maquiladora murders
young girls left crumpled, braids cut off
bits of pay slips found under pink nails
they warn of an invisible plague that has invaded my mother
red armies taking over honest cells.

Glaring pixels blind eyes too tired to sleep
as the dial up begins my fingers lament the deserts between us
under each key a child's skull from the graves of Monzote
under each rock the echo of two 4th graders at war
their scissors still chasing each other around Room 11
with a hate as open and hungry as the Grand Canyon.

My sweet unconditional,
what of the woman who changed her name to Lola
boarded a Greyhound and crossed state-after-state to see
if she'd make the same mistakes as far from him as she could get
and what of lovers hunted by mosquitoes in Managua
their dark flesh hidden by banana leaves
depressed breezes flirting with their nipples
will the scars of their scratching show come dawn?

What of the screams of the mute
do they leave from the eyes
and do those same eyes extract memory from tears
enough to start a new blue planet
those piercing red layers of granite between us
like the painted walls of Palenque
what amount of dynamite would it take to break into a heart that stiff?

My sweet unconditional,
there is no one to send these questions to but you

tonight an anonymous brick went through the window of Mr. Lim's market
landing one shoplifter dead.
My love do curses brand the same in Korean
and if they do where can we market this rage?
There is sadness at 3 a.m. at 4 and at 5
there is dawn then duty
pinned to my mattress
tattooed to last night's neck
spelled in pink crosses along the ravine
our love, an s.o.s. straddled over time.

OVER PASS-T DUE CONFESSION

I.

Under the overpass two boys walked
parading gold-dipped silver chains
breast plate crosses & Nike signs, size of sunspots
enough to catch the eye of our would-be leader

II.

I knew the short one from Kindergarten
where we shared a box
his name on top
and I'd hated him for it

a good girl would have looked away
when the tall one's veins burst
frightened moons covered with webs of red licorice
a good girl would have ran when his kneecaps shattered
sound like lunar rover landing

III.

today there are HBO specials
that could make this suburban horror real for you non-believers
this perennial fuck you at the hand of a practice bat
from have not to have less fools

IV.

"e'ry-body deserves a good beat down once in awhile"
that's what they told me and that's what I sold my God
after all *my man* was most beautiful when he'd hit his mark
and sad girls that want to stay happy learn to laugh shit off

V.

shamed I think of the sons I don't have
the ones I dare teach
wound collars of barbed wire nailed to their necks
an ancient scar size of dime bag
settle between their brow
I think of the Amor-all slide that made it easy
to jump in and get away

VI.

Hell is that they went on living
with grandma's waffles and football
to make the work week sweeter
they went on drinking at 4th St. Dicks
planning their revenge on napkins and place mats
but we were a faceless plague
spreading ourselves too thin

VII.

so I laughed the scales
up and down the white ivory of the poor bastard's teeth
my apologies for having nothing better to do that night
than hold my man's chain
while he worked out his rage on the face of someone else's brother

RICO SUAVE

Rico *Suave* liked to lick muñeca virgins
enough to get them loose
and when they closed their eyes
he would slip
bonitas
queridas
and *suavecitas*
down their skirts
let the bass in his Camero do most of the work
while his hands kept time on drumskin hips
their breast like burial mounds
pressed against his black curls
they'd kiss
taste God
swear faith
flower panties drop to the floor
knees deep in zebra print
Suave, el santo, reclined on his throne
a crushed velvet cushion to lean on
while pushing religion down their throats.

THE PREACHER AT VICTORY OUTREACH
SPEAKS TO SAVE MY HOMEBOY'S SOUL

Sinner beware!!
Submit your sin at the feet of Jesus
polish God's shoes with your retired rag
run boys, run round the snake-charmed congregation
your arms raised and chest cocked like Black Mambo.

Spread the word children
with razor sharp prayers let the world know
the homeboy crusade is coming
high as bonfire flame
aiming for your Saturdays and Mondays
in between days
claiming your families as their own.

Visitors, slouching in the back row
we see you, sloppy with the Devil's lies
we've known you as temptation
but not this time
today you are in *Our* house.

My sons, know you are here to suffer
let me carve out your tattoos
letter by letter
until the warrior has been scarred over
until you are a callous of regret and misguided good intentions.

Get a job good citizen
break the Lord off some pocket change
there is Kool-Aid and donuts in the vestibule for members.
Did you bring your ID?
Have your children memorized their Psalm?
Is your wife alone at home?

Brothers, we'll bail you out of your spiritual prison
we'll mortgage your soul
come, lend me your hand
let the Holy Spirit take hold your tongue
don't fight the work of redemption
there is a Heaven right here on Earth
and Vatos are more than welcome.

YARD SALE MAMACITA
Guest starring la Chismosa

I.

The art of language is a white prom dress sprawled on the floor.

Sequins dug deep into old shag
leave you to house-wife luxuries
telenovelas, microwave home cooking and canned frijoles
when the old man lays down
3.50 an hour times sixty
you smile sweet like fifteen
reassure him with your tone
claro mi corazon es suficiente
sometimes you lie to make ends meet.

Two bags in each hand
ankles swollen like summer tics
you waddle from stop sign to stop sign
a dozen eggs, tortillas, crossword book
no one knows the young girl genius
who won the Pomona Elementary Spelling Bee *five times*
no one knows how you once wore a size six
don't you know everyone is beautiful on prom night.

II.

Aches you are too proud to let go
settle into your back like son #1
you stay buried in a Korean blanket
from a sunken sofa you zone into and out of old photos
framed and nailed to the wall
each an altar to the possibilities that haunt you
hijo querido #2 would have come home
had he never called that recruiter back
y el pendejo still calls after son #3
who sits down to do his matemáticas

cause on day he's gonna build you a bridge to paradise
made from foil, cebolla and an endless mile of sunshine.

III.

You tell Lydia, *nosy mujer*
who lives alone with twenty cats next door
that you are of Spanish descent, *una gitana*
you tell her so well, even you start to believe your own lies
a Flamenco firefly
you twirl around a 1972 vacuum
that long since choked on pennies
change best spent on visiting days too far to bus to
6 a.m. to 5 p.m.
yard sale lady
a.k.a. "mamá" "vieja" "mi mujer"
prom queen figure for sale
synched tight round the mannequin's waist
you wait for someone to be blinded by its flat light
hold your breath when it sells for thirty billetes
to la viejita loca, the one crippled in her feet
and as wide as two tires round her waist
she says she will save it for her granddaughter
la que nunca visita.

Here, where only the wind remembers you
bella... vestida de sueños sequins y juventud
she whispers lavender blessings
that make this day more bearable than most.

SUNDAY MOURNING OVER
HUEVOS RANCHEROS

another red summer burns your intestines
as you scoop sunshine with limp tortilla
from my kitchen seat I imagine the tubes that kept you alive
each a garden snake in Adam's Eden

your father stretched over the guitar
his mother left him under a broken street lamp
in Ensenada he'd play til his fingers bled
calling her to come home

at the door twin witnesses claim Jehovah is waiting
for your mother faith's a full book of matches
each votive a hungry totem
in her life there have been two kinds of men...

...those that die and those that haven't yet

I know how tight the Reaper holds you
how he buried your umbilical cord in his backyard
like a voodoo curse your carry lead in your belly
tatted prayer hands mask holes in your back

this Sunday there are fresh haircuts to get
a single file line of remaining friends
pallbearers with number in hand
waiting for the Barber to drop his scythe

VIGIL

On the corner of Figueroa & Citron
a lady sits wrapped in black lace
twenty-four candles at her feet
I should not know the number but I do.

As I pass her my speed drops to a crawl
I've fallen into a grave and she is looking down at me
her long black braid a sure rope.

I pull myself up to stand next to her
death stains my chest
glass slivers dug deep into cheeks that no longer bleed
my hands are limp salamanders
my legs rooted lichen.

Together we stare this angel down
her eyes made up with cotton candy blue
a white cotton dress
silent smile tucked away
that day she was late
her class in urban planning started at 6 p.m.
at 5:25 a mid-sized sedan took an accelerated ride
through her cross street
leaving her a mangled web of pages and skin.

For twenty-four days her mother prayed us into slow motion
her sorrow ruled that corner
her child had cities to build
violins to make sing
now parks grow from her feet
and whole blocks are cluttered landscapes of chalk outlines.

On those Saturday nights when SUVs barrel down the center lane
taking out trash cans and strays
those nights when I drive my sober ass home

wailing like a dove set free from a Jalisco jail
I see the victims of impatience lining the road
and I know it should not move this fast
this passing should catch our breath
if only for the length of a light.

HANDBALL IN LINCOLN HEIGHTS

one hundred fifty-eight roaches between my bare feet and the bathroom
twenty-one cold steps from this heap of dusty orange sheets
this must be where the police will find me
smiling like good time girls do right after they've been caught

twenty-one colds steps between my bare feet and the bathroom
at 2 a.m. Lincoln Heights needs lip gloss
why can't I smile like good time girls do right after
in these hills my cell don't work, I am disconnected

2 a.m. and a girl needs lip gloss
what do lovers in favelas do for kicks
no reception, disconnected 1st world bitch
good time girl to the nth degree

this must be what lovers in favelas do for kicks
swat palmetto bugs in makeshift handball courts
good times under cover of stained sheets, 1st world retreat
legacy of bolder women's feet worn in the tile of his abuela's floor

palmetto bug handball
must be where the last girl gave up
the sight of his abuela swatting then stomping tile floor
beady-eyed monsters retreat to the corner

standing where the last girl gave up
scared to wet myself, the sheets, abuela's tile floor
I did not come here to dance with roaches while my hillside gangster sleeps
beady-eyed monster, his legs up in the air

this must be where I come to my senses
find my shoes, pretty pink tanga, entrails of my dignity
run past abuela and out the front door
but being good time to the nth degree
I curl back into the warm body between me and my great expectations

KILLING IS WHAT HE WAS BORN TO DO

like some are born to paint
or pitch or risk their lives for some worthy cause
look miss, a poem just like you like
about real shit miss,
real like OGs get down for
his enemy's lung an impaled birthday balloon hung on the fence
red lint on white of his cap and kicks
revenge for a life of blank pages.

Being teacher I'd asked for a poem
about a memory they couldn't forget
a first kiss
a first hit from their old man
maybe their first trip to the beach
something real that they could still see
when they closed their eyes at night
like light on your corneas after the switch has been pulled down
the ardent echo of something there before.

It was an epic poem for his trigger finger
crescent moon of right thumb
pink from the squeeze
he'd made so many
their eyes like moths under streetlights
silent nods of homeboys piled in bucket seats
the ride back to the crib
where enchiladas were waiting
taste of ash and blood and beans
mud between this death and the others.

He was born to kill,
like only real thugs can
like only real teachers can comprehend
what it's like to shoot an open ended question into a storm cloud.

THANKSGIVING WITH SIN

Sin, he black eye of domino
father Blood
born on backside of industry
end of freeway 5
where Mac trucks clutter veins like clots

at midnight his mother counts alien ships
from her lawn chair
Keith Sweat serenading the block
where Sin, part devil, part man lives
under halo of urban myth

see Sin, under my skin
his kind of brown like Mississippi mud on my stretch marks
like bits of rust under my nails from swing set sessions
after strip poker and two liters of Old English

Sin, ever thankful
sets me and mamma to steamin at 4 a.m.
collards and yams
not even he will eat
turkey meat stuck in my throat
cause Sin don't date skinny girls
cause his babies sit to my right and left

today Sin both father and son
lazy-eyed martyr of a real G's life after all debts been collected
and when I want to play Bonnie to his Clyde
Sin sits up straight
tells me, *this ain't no life for a good girl*
no kind of life at all
but I know all the words to Mr. Sweat's songs
and how to season greens
how to yell domino with as much fire as ice
bet I know how to make any man happy

Sin, now father and politician
kisses my baby fat
takes me by the hand and smacks my ass on my way out
sayin, *good girl you go on home*
before you catch yourself believing you belong

JAMIE

eyes tied back with black lightening
charcoal rope braided behind her
with pomegranate lips split open, Jamie
could not say no.

While we, the restless, went fishing for richer men
she'd wait by the phone
the calls always came at 7 or 10
Lady, do you accept the collect charges?
yes, she said
yes again and again to the men we'd forgotten
yes to men we'd outgrow before their parole.

There was Juan who liked grape soda and dominoes on Sunday.
Tito who smelled like the cologne aisle in Macy's.
Bobby who never knew when to stop laughing.
Wilson with his tired one line,
"Hey baby, did you hurt yourself fallin from heaven?"
and Sweet Tyrone who could outrun the track team of the school
that asked him to leave when he wouldn't return his history book.

Jamie never said no to their speeches
their poems carved on the wall
their requests for more cigarettes more cash more letters
Jamie stayed home chasing away the high gray waves of solitary
but on some nights the waves won
and when we got home Jamie's lightening had run
down her cheeks a flood of black ink.

Guilty of abandoning our loves for good times
we'd dip our fingers in her stained sink
write of how our love would never end
that we'd wait until the Second Coming
for a second chance to hold them again
we'd promise a letter a night
until the warden had drowned in our pages.

Then the days would unwind like hot rollers
and our lips would cry out for shock red
good times would seep out from the radio and back under our skin
but Jamie she stayed on to carry our tears for us
and when I think of women most loved
by wind by storm by ink

I think of Jamie, eyes tied with black lightening
charcoal rope braided behind
her pomegranate lips on the seals of crisp envelopes
buoys for men lost at sea.

A LOVE POEM FOR A HATE CRIME VICTIM SPREAD OVER THE MALIBU HILLS

twisted bullets thrown up into a sky too blue to hold heaven

seeds bursting with vermilion of lips yet to be kissed

eyes swollen from poison sprays melted into these mountain ranges

here, wanderers wind like rain down paths made by those who dared
        to swallow *lost* whole

let hunger worm its way through their pot bellied bodies like
        an unpolished hollow tip split into clover

clawing through sands fallen through figurine of God's time

born under mosaic arches of the Alhambra

wounded and healing in Nazi, California

hidden thirteen miles below this sea

thirteen years deep into lifelines they cut

and thirteen months later I'm still watching you bleed

Zapata brava bloodstains on orange buttercups

Your aches loiter on stones cut perfect for resting
        by sunlight and patience

can't you see your pain is nesting itself into my poetry

a lone summit on why free trade isn't really free

a hungry pipe bomb left where our unborn baby sleeps

a sickle cell on the back of a dead man's pillow

spreading still through the echo of air force jets

the hum of ancient regrets   over   bound   towards
        a mountain we too faded to climb

love enters swaying lazy like peacebreakbeat on ranchera time

slicing still through streets with names that sound plain dumb in
        Webster framed English

oh baby you do this   with your wind   your easy way

you do this and I know   if I leave   it won't be today.

BURNT BRIDGES

Behold, how great a matter a little fire kindled.
And the tongue is a fire,
a world of iniquity:
so is the tongue among our members.

JAMES III v.5-6

BATTLE

It has been eight months
since I've looked into the toilet bowl
and seen my reflection spitting up all that is good in me
piercing my thorax with bitten nubs
blunted by years of acid reflux
index and middle worked so consistently
they now host incomplete ovals
where my identity seeped out one meal at a time.

In my locker I kept the books
no one thought it would occur to me to read.
In my house I kept score of who was winning the war,
my mother or me.
You'd think she would've noticed the cover up
water running, leftovers left on the plate
but she was busy reclaiming her body
putting on pounds he had denied her for years
it was fear that kept her bird boned and emptied.

In Psych 101 they say it is a white girl's disease
brought on by years of exposure to Vogue
sour lilies on a waif mother's vanity
a tea party of sunken skeletons
working their way through skin with gossip and tweezers
and maybe it was the white girl in me wishing her way to the front
through the layers of hip and sway
to the front where college recruiters could see her
all blonde and lean and shake her hand
without fear of contamination.

And maybe it is the white girl who is lonely now
that there are no ulcers guarding her burden
lost she wanders the mountain ranges of my body
wondering when I let go

but I know better
this battle is old habit
one like any other racist twitch
and it lives in the repetition of unloving everything we are
starving all cells equally until you become something other than yourself.

PARKING ON THE EVE OF MORE BAD NEWS

you haven't given into the forty-ounce yet
moaning when you blow on its neck just right
for tonight you make do with skin
for tonight I'm aloe vera stretched over your belly of scars

before love there are doctors
spirits and dead nerves between us
clogging pores, staining our lives like iodine
for tonight we make do with skin

though I know the dosage it takes to light the inside
I haven't given into the bottle yet
moaning when you blow on its neck just right
for tonight I take sips full of wind

if there is more to this cliff
this edge of the world romance
more than dead ends and scarred flesh
let it be found in the stars
a sacred code
charted and passed on for generations
a scroll tucked inside bottle
with news of a lost pair
in search of new skin to love with

ODE TO AN ESTRANGED LAX

Having lost my tribe,
I'd come here seeking Rosa Carmina's face in late night arrivals
someone always hugging, crying, goodbyeing
a census of parallel lives
where any rolling stone could leave at will
stretch arms, tilt hat, wave ticket and take off into the next.

I needed to know you'd never shut me out.

Now we threaten you,
must relinquish all emotion just to stand in line
with no one holding hands
everyone steaming in the ash of an unthinkable fate
pay phone receiver confirming
beyond metal detectors and unexpected frisks
in a land of dormant volcanoes
in a night of fainting blue skies
awaits one sweet melon ball kiss.

UNDER THE BRIDGE

His face a cactus paddle
arms and legs—stumps of an olive tree
the school sent a warning letter
she reads it to the mirror

behind stumps of an olive tree
the boogieman lives!
warnings left in lipstick on the bathroom mirror
she believes someone will believe

the boogieman lives,
in a manila file, under a hundred such files
she believes someone will believe
the girls in their mini-skirts, their faces made-up, shoulders bare to the sun

a hundred such files on a desk held hostage by 2nd class victims
she wipes his spit off her neck
her mini-skirt torn, mascara smeared, bruised shoulders bare to the sun
she claws her skin until there is nothing left

she wipes his spit off her neck
inside the boogieman growing
the red headed nurse holds her hand while the doctor scrapes
             until there is nothing left
under the bridge but a gym bag and broken shoe lace

inside her—an egg covered in spines
a bell rings, freeing an endless trail of 16-year-old girls
pink sweaters and pumas with fat laces
the number 2 bus with stops just after the bridge

an endless trail of girls, most walking home alone
his change swallowed by money slot
the number 2 bus with stops just after the bridge
her scars testimony, the boogie man lives.

EXIT STAGE LEFT

You, my love, are lonely
because we with spray can proverbs
have gradually made their sonnets our own
we their most aggravated wound
have taken this treasured jewel
and polished it with black soap.

You interview the dead on open mics
more secure in spotlights than séances
ask out loud where a brother can score in this town
to weather this tempest of addictions
we tour sketches of sidewalk artists
hold our ears to the wind for news of island babies
survivors of shark-infested seas
landed on jagged concrete of this New Spain.

Loving you is the first hit
lips tight round a glass river
I wonder what we'll make with the smoke and
how many turns each will take before passing?

If life has ever failed you
then know not to plant me in your heart
for I would grow there too fast
pulsing in asthmatic sensitivities
each breath a refugee from the high life
under red velvet of my sex.

My sweet unconditional, exit stage left
no song could save you from the orgy of oxtails and old habits
no summer rain could remove your ink stain from my lips.

HOUR GLASS

I. 1995

From where to where we've come and still so far from home.
I call you to be heard but you are too proud to listen.
You call me to advise but all I hear are the mad ramblings of a woman
who has turned her back on that brown baby
once stuck to her pink breasts.
This routine as much family as physics and bombs
more related than up is to down
more codependent than codeine & flu
I scream I AM through the phone, then hang myself
on the umbilical cord wrapped around her version and mine.

II. 1999

I send slides of my DNA so she can see
there is no way to avoid this life she claims I've chosen
but logic concludes with Hello
instead we discuss musicals
sing a hymn or two from *The King and I*
and for a moment there is harmony
then I remember there are Asian stereotypes
and negative feudalistic subplots to consider
I have crossed the line this time for sure
Hammerstein is choking me and Rogers is breaking through my front door
while she pounds out reasons why I am...
an unfit American, a terrible citizen, my rent late,
my car illegal, my man unemployed, my credit in ruins...
though I can't see the mess I've made
I know she is boiling over and my heart skips beats
because it knows I am no longer her little girl
and that's when we both get the point.

III. 2006

I exit a burning Los Angeles on a magic tax return check
a gallon of gasoline in one hand and pen in the other
for five months she has held in every tear
cause she is Virgo and they don't lose well
even the doctors tell me how competitive she made the last days
a race between her spit and the lymphoma
not even my rage can get me there in time
like her I refuse to cry but there is sand in my chest
in my throat building up into tumors
it takes me years to spell *I am sorry* with single grains
and just seconds for her to sweep them all away.

YOUR ISLAND

nighttime in your mother's bed is a marathon of creed
incessant chirping of coquis
abusive rain on tin rooftop
knowing you'd rather miss your island than own her

in four hours you'll call to say you're not the one
that no mystic could tap the vein to your heart

the choir only hears what they want
your drum calling Eleggua to open phlegmatic chords
hands rough from digging in other men's yards
gently tracing my pink shell
your beard's broken needles scratching
worn 45 of my laugh lines
the slow roll of a homemade cassette
your boleros holding the air hostage like you never left

BLOOD

Your boy asks where you go when you are gone
you point to a black hole only a dead man could see
there son, in-between God's eyes.

Did you think of him when you held out your arm
fist tight green veins throbbing with another punch of anthrax?
Does poison pass from father to son?

While other men saw naked angels
carved in crude oil skies
you saw healthy kidneys
two pair
one for yourself
one for your father
the man whose hands held bottles before they held yours
stumbling up rock past waterfalls and prehistoric trees
he led you up summits of el Yunque
asleep against a stump while you counted stars.

When they called your name did you know how far you'd travel
and what color you'd have to kill?
Did the blood of "sandniggahs" spill into your dreams?

High from a scorpion's kiss at night you'd see Yemaya rise
above the tanks and sleeping men
her hands cupping a turquoise sea
your son at the bottom
asleep on a bed of chicken bones.

Did you own your hate when they told you
there was nothing wrong with your body?
no toxic verve seeping from your hand to his
no pill to keep the grains of sand from filling your lungs.
At the observatory he has his own story for each light
his own reasons to survive
he has found you wounded but willing to ask for his help.

FOR THE FLOWER WOMEN

For years the family has called to tell of deaths that couldn't wait
of flower women who could no longer breathe stained air of memory
women woven of chichicaste and mud, spotted with age
alone in houses loitered by grandchildren
who still feed off sagged breasts
as steam from clay pot clings to their faces
like responsibility of having to feed one more.

The phone call is made by some cousin
who would have been brother or sister had they been closer
tired from the wake and scared to practice their English in post-mortem dialogue
we stumble together through fields of fiber optic cables
as to arrange payment of headstone, scent and color of flower,
        dress of beloved.

My father numbed by distance no longer cries
and so I ambassador to the past he's long-since entombed
navigate the river balanced on a worn cross
bobbing between one shore and the other.

It's the absence of the land that won't let me forget
her hand's ritual preparing té de canela
raised veins rubbing herbs and crèmes into my hair
the women who always had time to *pray first M'ija, always pray first.*

Now lying still, a balsa wood figurine of what I would have been
had I been born before convenience
what we the modern nameless warless childless
generation of cracked bridges are
when no one sees our heads bowed before altars we once mocked
twisted beads between bitten nails, lips tucked under with mumbled penance
feigning faith long enough to know with her dies the kind of woman
who lifts tortillas out of sand, shapes them into hearts
fills our bellies on sacrifice and with a kiss
promises tomorrow there will be more than enough.

THE ROSARY

when we make love it hangs on the bedpost
a noose stained brown by blood
a muddy river's overflow
you hold it when you drive
when we kiss your fist always between our chests
our arteries sense the history and crawl
like vines to touch salvation's erect x

on national ditch day I make us a picnic
cheezits chicharrones grapes
small plastic plates and napkins folded like cranes
a skill you say makes you believe in Pangea

instead our holiday is spent in search of the thin rope
knotted by a blind nun
one for each blip in the flatline that was your life
—you promised Him—her prayers would not go in vain
at sundown I sit on the balcony and eat without you
while you dig through my dirty underwear like Pilate's men
hunting for a trace of flesh in the shroud

ON DEFINING US

ABANDONADO, ABANDONAR, ABAJO
you were gonna teach yourself Spanish
while I was in my Don Quixote lecture
legs crossed, eyes intent on absorbing the "A" section
of my Spanish-English Dictionary
the words you choose to learn

ABANDONADO-ABANDONED, DESERTED
ABANDONAR-TO QUIT, GIVE UP
ABAJO-BELOW, DOWN

abajo tu vives
abandonado y abandono
I thought your curiosity cute
but you were not looking for a new tongue to love with
you were looking for another way to say "I quit."

HOW I LOST MY FATHER TO AMERICA*

He was there for the length of El Bigote's grito
GOOOOAAALLLLLL!
and then just like that he'd fade
into another hour-long patience
awaiting the next great angle
I'd wait with him
2,000 miles away in a sagging futon
watching a borrowed TV
that never received team *America* in full pixel form
hopeful as Cuahtemoc's granddaughter
that someday these cleated warriors would grow feathers
fly back in time to when winners were sacrificed
to when one strike of the stone ball
meant seizure or sudden death
back to when the stake's were too high
to hold my father's attention.

Without notice he stopped calling
on Sundays at 8 a.m.
and again at 9
he stopped calling on holidays, birthdays
and in-between days when he does what men do
when they have been left by their everything.

Thought it was my engagement to a communist
that left him speechless under sable palm
waiting for legitimate grandchildren to call on him to play
reason enough to try him after six months
on Sunday at 8 a.m.
and again at 9.

Listening more to El Bigote's grito
than to my innocuous good news
(como'tas papa) bien bien m'ija

y tu? (bien) okay good I love you
pray to Jesus (I pray dad, I pray)
Good (espera papá tengo noticias)
hum okay I love you Good
GOOOOAAALLLLLL!!!! (bye)

*America is the state soccer team of Guadalajara, Mexico

DON'T MESS WITH THE BULL

La Zona Rosa, Mexico, D.F.

Jesus is the cousin that makes being cousins hard
he's Infante without the mustache
a certified hottie
he is policeman and rebel
responsible and cruel
my ideal man
my adopted big brother

he forbids me to ride
the electric bull lonely and waiting
says only a puta would be so crass
so I wait for him to go to the restroom
tie my skirt high around my hips
and mount the dormant beast

this is for las adelitas! I cry
que viva la bruja, soldada, puta!
with an ay, ay, ay! thrown in for good measure
when he comes out drying his hands on his jeans
only to see me gyrating before the world
his friends making bets on how long I'll last
it's like I've wrangled his balls
he tackles
knocks me right off the bull
into the hay
into his arms

when he puts ice on my swollen ankle the next day
he swears my bruises prove him right
that there are some lessons only a man can teach

THE HOLY TRINITY AS DEPICTED IN WEST SIDE STORY

I like to live in America
Okay by me in America
Everyone free in America

I am Anita, mambo high at midnight
sweaty after a private rumble with a man I'd like to call my own
there are nights he calls for my legs only
hung over balcony like peace flags
then there are nights when I turn a blind eye to the war
only to wake my back a field of landmines & lesions
to survive you must love the fighter as much as the fight
sirens remind of a country that turns boys to assassins
no border could impede his ominous crusade
he's seen his village torched
his brother's tongue cut out
his baby aborted by the enemy's dirty blade
I am a red light salve on a wound America won't claim
but I say send me her newly-arrived vipers and thugs
I want to love them in triplicate.

America
Sweet America

I am Maria, mother of convicted killer
morning dove before God
my wings resting on oak
candles nestled in my hair
I paid for his passage with my body
exchanged his health for mine
paid for his uniform with tithes
saved from the months I was too ashamed to attend
waited up nights to see him stumble in bloody
his Sunday shirt torn
I never taught him to kill, but he learned just the same

before guns there was a mother's love
in line at the market I saw her, the other mother
she threw fruit at me and screamed, "madre del diablo"
I know who took her son and mine
it was the man who sticks needles in
prods them until there is nothing left but acid and black tongue.

America
Sweet America

I am the dress that made you look
that brought you home when you could've been out
when you could've been next
I am the satin on your skin
that asked you to dance with your finger tips not your fists
the curve and line that made you forget
for me you will pray to a God you thought had forgotten you
only he is a She and She is bombshell if you can see her
mother if you'll obey her
sister if you must devote your wars to someone's honor
at the end of night I will spin over you
dead set on delaying the last dance
a parasol of razor blades
a vow of tender flesh
a silk thread around your neck.

GOODNIGHT MOON

there was no moon the night I spent $43.50 in long distance charges
to hear you tell all the reasons I'd already heard
from my godmother my government
on why Cubans and Americans should never meet

there was no light when I left your letters
broken sacraments at the door of the only Orthodox Church
that still believes enough in God to leave its gates open at 3 a.m.

there was no silence high enough to block the celestial hum
the universal "I told you so" ringing like church bells in my hung-over heart
there was no answer no wind no you

I drew what I remembered of your face on the steamed stained glass
a map to where we left our hand prints
like an army of doves dipped in blue paint
enough to protect our nest in Trinidad
where we dared to plant wartime possibilities

your goodbye a reminder
never again will a line be open enough between us
for me to accept collect charges from your particular revolutionary star

LA BELLE BALLERINA

Like Scarlet she will not go quietly
she argues with specialists over words like "terminal" and "treatment options"
her bald head a blotchy map of resistance
the remaining hairs thin splinters of trees left after the Bomb
she pushes the nurse's hand away and promises the doctor this is not over
at home she feeds the cat, talks back to the president elect
she decides what we'll have for dinner, then too sick to join us
she retires to catch the last hour of another American Movie Classic.

In the bed where she read credits as they scrolled over her swollen womb
I catch her laughing
as technicolor lovers fight over who to invite to the ball
I take her feet in my hands
spread the tired bone and skin
massaging reminders of the nights it was her gown spinning
and the world went drunk with her grace.

TOMBSTONE INSCRIPTION FOR A LOVER ON 115TH

When you left
I never bothered
To take the sign off your back
That read// Recovering addict
Do not disturb
W/flightless
Love things
It would only bring
Bruises//

SIZE 10
for Nehanda

exile in Havana means
your shoe collection retreats into the closet of a Harlem apartment
you once rented when times were good

in your absence we've won
arguments on identity
perched on love seats
sipping ginseng teas
flirting with affirmative action
still sprung on what it's done for us
never stretched far enough to snap back

you'd smile and say *black*
baby, that's all you got
lift your left fist to your lips
and mumble COINTELPRO

photos of your lover, Mario
remind me of JJ from Good Times
his broad-toothed smile has you open
loose like New Years 1979
but in his grip I see you twisted
a squeeze of lime into warm rum
needing love like every woman do
holding tight like every mamma do

Ms. Dalton, I see you fly past in a U-Haul truck
you took four years to find your way to that island
your baby girl crying out for a reason she could touch on
why liberation for the People meant mommy's never coming home

they say you live it
live it like a Cuban
live it like you need it
cause maybe you do
a burst of superwoman
in and out of sweaty rooms
spilling a little secret here or there
so no one forgets what you gave

you Cherí Amour are grandmother to a beautiful ward
she, like yours and the fists before
lost in choices no sane women should have to make
from fifteen stories high you yell *Happy New Year!*

I came here to shop for feet I've only seen run
two for one at Payless
cause mamma you sho'nuff lived up to your size ten

SO AND SO

when we were children
my friend Lisa, the Baptist
told us suicide meant Hell for those who dared
to slice or swallow their way out of His grace
I told her to go to Hell cause my cousin was in Heaven
right where she belonged

when we were children
Charita came to my sleepovers
braided Lisa's hair into cherry-sized knots
and sang us all Bobby Brown's prerogative
in the morning she'd go back to the Southside of town
where Africa had settled 200 years ago against its will

when we were children
Central Avenue might as well have been the equator
slicing through our bicycle routes like crime scene tape
making us as curious as we were scared to cross
over the years we'd grow into strangers
shadows of an original hate
we could not remember why
we were no longer giggles in unison
when corn popped out of kettle into our wide-opened mouths
we could no longer remember when the doors to our houses
became steel plates between the nations taking cover from each other

rumors spread round those who know
you used to know so and so
and so I heard Charita was now a dancer
pumping hard at night
by the dim lights of club Atlantis
where baseball players doubled as pimps
for dentistry students and single mothers

rumors spread round those who know
you used to know so and so
and so I heard Lisa traded in Sunday school
for keg stands and best friends
who all called her whore
when number 54 said it was her with him and number 23
behind the bleachers she'd bleed onto her white pom pom shorts

and when I heard what I heard
I didn't defend the two loose-toothed girls
I'd once told all my secrets to cause I knew
they knew what they'd heard on me too
how I was a gang-girl now
bandanna beat downs to my credit
how I lost my virginity playing spades in an alley
where runaways converged to plan the next 7-11 heist

looking back it's hollow how
we came to trade each other in on slave blocks
outbidding with rumors of masters we'd conquer
someday I'm gonna pop some corn
and send my baby to deliver it on her two-wheel ocean blue bike
to the houses where we used to sleep side by side like sisters

LAUNDRY WITHOUT YOU

bald Colombian men argue over the referees call
how they would have made that shot
these men forced to come to this country alone
sentenced by war to do their own wash
trip over my scattered load
as they reenact the goal with a crushed coke can
the mamacitas with their hair in rollers
laugh extra loud at the pile of egos on the floor

could not tell you the benefits of liquid to powder
or if beige could be teamed with the whites
soon suds consume the room
tios slip, abuelas curse, babies cry
the Filipino manager waves his cane and screams *mamatay dyablo!*
ready to slay the machine with an up-set stomach
now a three-headed monster daring us to come closer

as I bob by the donut store
an empty detergent bottle my buoy
sea foam extended from Elysian to Virgil
I note Chapter 10 in the Illiad of my life without you
is as sad as Chapters 9 and 5
the ones where I tried to wax the car and tenderize the meat
the ones where I slid off the hood down the hill
covered in garlic salt and soy

without you I have no domestic role model
no iron man chef or certified buffer
I'm missing you like San Quentin misses tits and ass
crying into fabric softeners
yeah, missing you like that, damn

TUESDAY NIGHT AT KING KING'S

for two days after I saw you
maraca clave then rum
in your hands I'd sweat lava
working my skin into blisters
I never minded
the mirrors
the ice
never asked where you were before
or where you'd go after
as long as you came

for two days after you sang
sabia que ibas a llegar
I answered each ring
expecting to hear you missed me most at lunch
midday under a bitter sun
still it was enough to dance
under your nose
with his name I've forgotten
how much I hated
hibiscus wilted behind my ear
I'd hear the rumors of your conquests and laugh up blood

pride is an island—more hell then oasis
still I missed you and you knew it
damned I went on dancing
with his name I've forgotten
the exact extent of my rage
framed by your taino afro
challenging gravity
your lips swollen with song
mocking me still
sabia que ibas a llegar

"I knew you'd come" and I did
fists first, you kissed the knuckles
then flame, you lit the candles
then spit, you filled the glasses and toasted our love

tonight the good girl is leaving early
hands full of maraca clave then rum
back steaming from the pace of the mambo
head held high this time
hibiscus coaching
don't look back
and I won't
not even when you call my name
mid-song, center stage
and that is worth the price of admission

TESTED

the pipe sighed before it gave way to the weight of the Federale's boot
long and worn it sighed the way a woman does when her man is explaining
why he must leave we were fifteen miles from the border five hours from
crossing eight from home the activist in me thought it unjust a waste of
a perfect pipe the night before cheap wine and moon Ensenada full of salt-
water puddles the licking between us the jagged line between moon and sea
they wanted me in exchange for your freedom their smiles filled with silver
their tongues forked with the thought of the trade laughing at my white girl
English (the kind I turn on when I most want to know the truth about men)
they made you do push-ups two hundred and thirty-one for each mile we'd
traveled to escape ourselves and the ending we'd promised we'd never let
happen your arms heavy with the weight of your duty to protect the sigh of
your chest under the Federale's boot a reminder that love is not the shadows
we left dancing by the fireplace but a showdown between us and the world

TESTED II

what does it matter, positive or negative
my cells have a secret to tell

what does it matter that I knew you a lifetime or one night
that a simple question could have evaded this wait

what does it matter, when in the moment precious is as she does
and she does what she wants regardless

what does it matter, this endless week at Lammle's, Borders, the page
celebrating the flutter of everyday

what does it matter, the answer
if Eve has already taken her bite of infinite sin
and being great-granddaughter there can be no hope for me

what does it matter, the answer behind that door
in a room filled with Kleenex and cushions
in case I don't take the news well

what does it matter, the nurses are on lunch, all except one
t matters to her that I know before the worry on my fingertips spreads
ɔm one magazine to the next

what do you care that on the way home there is only Springsteen
ʰat I've known every word since birth
't start a fire without a spark

; it matter that he's right
ˋ survived another day
skipped over by the wild flames

atter when the house of my neighbor will still burn

TESTED III

cacophony — the sound of a 4th grade music class

disingenuous — me the last time I took on a Puerto Rican drummer

harangue — my mother on finding out about said Puerto Rican drummer

fell — he fell my heart like a lumberjack in a sacred forest, no one heard
the crash but me

plunder — I plunder through the sales rack to work through the ache

these words borne by the mouths of men I never trusted
branded into my brain with each repetition
with each florescent flash card
closer to 600

"You must improve two hundred percent to be considered for our program,"
must twist and tame tongue to this foreign vocabulary
this multi-syllabic regime of founding fathers

it's Friday night
the kitchen staff is cleaning
their salsa beats tug at my feet
stuck in the drill of ages
proof of worth
scale of words
Oxford has swollen my tongue
tongue that would rather kiss
spout poems or talk shit
it is 10:35 p.m. and there is no end
to the droning academic klan in my head
I deny them their last words, reclaim my day
and slip away in grooves on the floor

WHY I LEFT WITHOUT SAYING GOODBYE
for Ebony

my thesis on the teachings of Ghandi was left on the Greyhound
between Cambridge and Port Authority I'd let that prayer go
cornrows half in-half out, must have scared a few
laws of nature say, a lioness cannot be arrested for protecting her young
but the warrant was written anyway

at Harvard it's illegal to leave your hot comb on the stove
to play Tupac before noon or after six it's illegal
to eat out, laugh loud, ash your cigarette on the pretty red brick
jagged and awkward as two county beds we dared to stay on
but there were too many martyrs that summer
ghost fists eager to punch holes in hallowed halls

still see you in the mirror,
can sometimes feel your hold on my thick mane
wonder where you are and who you've trusted
if you ever left the Brenton Harbor projects again
swore it was all good so why Harvard burn still
in my chest water fountains soothe the public
and thirst is still free, ivy league burn bridges
but we   we   throw   bricks

PUNCH LINE

I. Meyer Lansky – the name of the Jewish Mafioso we couldn't remember at 2 a.m.
II. Muhammed Ali – a hero we can both claim
III. brick walls – why my head always aches after leaving you

After a night of you & Jack Daniels
a dream of myself in a chapel with Meyer Lansky & Muhammed Ali
brick walls topped with elaborate paintings of Heaven & Hell
dare devil anarchists suspended in a cockleshell
pace the room to find a crack in the wall
a million questions gather behind my teeth;
like how many angels did they see at the bell?
is there an afterlife after the fall?
could I walk away with my guard down?

Subdued by the steady stream of blue river above
the sneering red river below
Muhammed Ali, Meyer Lansky and me
sit suspended on wood chairs like lions
waiting for the punch line to crack its whip
we take turns saying the show will go on.

So this is love just before the straight jacket
the sting operation before your number's called
this is the hull of my heart throbbing with afterwords.

ON THE VERGE OF THE NEXT RIOT

the monster grill of a Mac truck in your rearview could cause panic

my lover is driving for the first time since he hit a tree
and took a well-deserved nap

it soothes him to know I know the songs on 93.1,
the classic *classic* rock station

how Pink Floyd & lasers suit me fine as Prince & pink lace

we agree the children still don't need no education, what they get
from concrete is enough

we interrupt this broadcast to bring you breaking news
on the Donovan Jackson case

a hung jury

another black boy beat down

two white cops balls big enough to cheer from their pews as if
taken by the Holy Spirit

education is winter on his auntie's TV screen

a faded buzz of more to come

valley of smog pierced with high wired toothpicks set up to receive
cell phone soliloquies

a halo of radiation 10 miles wide

20 million microwaves and me with one weak heart

tell it on the mountain, I'm on the road—again,
with a man who can't sing but sings still

tell the black boy, hands tied behind his back, face against the police car
reason has interfered

the city burns to burn behind us, it's desire channeled
by the matches in my pocket

will the willing pay $2.50 a gallon to turn back

at the next exit I cry for the aunties on their plastic sofas, the police
"just doing their job," the long- horned trucker
bullying his way through it all

OBSERVATION NOTES FROM THE NEW WORLD ORDER

Psst!, psst, psst!
Is anyone there? Anyone listening?
Someone looking? Even a heart?

SUBCOMANDANTE MARCOS

MISSING

"...for men must work
and women must weep
and there's little to earn
and many to keep
though the harbor bar be mourning"
–Charles Kingsley

Juan Abrego misses his wife
when he steps off the metro
and just before the wind hits his back
he can feel her breath on his fingers.

He misses his country
the green mountain
the stoic trees
the neighbors and their animals
underfed and overworked he misses most
the little girl with eyes as black as his
who smiles in her sleep
the swinging hammock
the sprawling song of his father's farm
field of corn where they first made love
the child bride and groom
he held her hand and promised not to take long
the vow between them sewing together the hours.

Today Juan Abrego wrote his first paragraph in English
my wife has eyes like twin stars
he has begun to translate the loss
how you say extrañar "missing"
how you say solo "alone".
Juan misses chasing the crows off his land
the uncles gathered to watch the game
a rock he touched everyday on his way home.

But, good luck does not reach this far.
You have to return to its source
my wife has skin like honey
my daughter is a dancing sparrow
the letter is read to the class
then sent with a crisp hundred dollar bill
each with their own envelope to fill
the life they left
the lone woman sowing the field
the black eyes hiding
the child grown tall as the stalks.

IN MONTAÑITA OLD AGE IS A GIFT

for the victims of crossfire

there are days when the daughters think to sit on the porch

sip the same lemonade

a brew of what's gone sour in life

instead they stay in

hold babies tight to their chests

it's best to lie still

pretend you are dead

so when the beast comes

he can roll you over

maul your face til it's a monster's mask

leave you wounded but living

to be old as Maria & Ismenia

you must survive more changes then men

they'd been friends since the rivers ran blue

spirit twins too busy reminiscing on first loves

to notice machine guns aiming at air

how Armando made love with a flower first

sending blood to her hand her arm her shoulder

how her lips trembled

yes, it was like that with Pedro

a jewelry box after only two months

the lock carved from alabaster

shock made her drop it

the gold ring calling to her from bits of wood and shell

he never got mad once in 56 years

they laid side by side

they'd escaped the violence so many times

found refuge in fields and churches

an endless string of prayers wound around each fist

taking watch over children's children

shooting goals between trash bins

it was milk she needed

for milk she sent her grandson to the store

maybe she knew to save him

glasses shattered

sunshine turned dusty rose

their lives mixing again

two swallows

struck down by skipping stones

CHRISTMAS DINNER 1997

The martyrs of Acteal have opened our eyes ...
they left us the truth as an inheritance ...we see
how there is no justice in Mexico ... we see how arms
have come to our communities ... and are given to
assassins ... all to strengthen an army that never tires
of taking over our lands and controlling our
populations."

> *—From a statement made by the*
> *Abejas at the year anniversary of the massacre*

we sit heads bowed
praying over an obese turkey
three snow white heads
and my brown mane
grateful to our Lord
for more stuffing more meat more gravy
light and dark we sit
juxtaposed like negatives

they chatter   avoid my eyes
I am *hysterical,* liberal dead weight tied to their North Star
each a Jeopardy contestant speaking with endless expertise
on campaign finance and the *corruption* of welfare
they chew unaffected by the ten-second news flash
on another massacre below our stretched first world belt

excuse me

I search suburban streets for the remains of fifteen harpooned placentas
fifteen mothers not given a choice between their lives or their children's

excuse me

alone in a strip mall parking lot
I mumble prayers for forgiveness through the filter of my black-n-mild
as visions of reckless machine guns dance through my head

excuse me

mother, it's true
I've never mashed the molcajete with their daughters
never carried my children through jungles deep in the night
vines tearing at my face
bouquet of fear trail enough for monsters
to bound close behind for five days

it's true   I was born here
not under their piece of sky
but that does not stop their faces
from burning like champa in my corneas
their screams from bursting my ear drums

tragedy does not pause for Christ's birthday
sadness is memory
of when time began
gave birth to man
and man took his hate
shot it into his shadow's heart
saying take that   take that   take that

NEW WORLD NEWSIE

Your village in El Salvador had no school
but you made it to 2nd grade anyway,
took a mountain path past five encampments
to stand at your desk and recite the tenets of the latest leader.

Farmer Diego brought paper from the city
a peso a sheet, pounded as thin as Mayan gold.
Once you sold your boots for a book
and the captain tied you to a tree for a week.
Oh, what kind of soldier you would have made
had you stayed on to see the revolution through.

Mr. New World Newsie, can you read the trouble you sell?
Nowadays fifty cents buys a world of pain.
You stand two seconds too long, daring the red light to go green
willing business men in sedans to drive through you.

You shove Spanish news—more blood than truth—in their window
switch hands and try English—more words than art—on the windshield
headlines stain your hands and sleeves.
Can you explain why so many don't want to know?

"Good" & "Evil" went to war today. Where's the news in that?
Once you miscounted your sales and they docked you a week's pay,
still you stood at Fairfax & Adams waiting for someone to ask your name.

HORIZONTAL GEOGRAPHY LESSON

your bed is the edge of the world
where we lie
unnumbered
unhinged
tracing the outline of your United States map

you're determined to know the state capitals and their order
rainbow quilt of stoic rhombi
how free the coastal states
their furthest seams defined only by volcano and sea

my index finger trails the Rio Grande
its mud bleeding down my chest
your thumb leaves coyote tracks
guides for those that follow

this land is ours

as the politicians sleep through our rebellion
we take back California for my grandfather
Louisiana for yours
here manifest destiny dare not brand its legend
arrows pointing toward an imagined west
a muted south a lonely east a frozen north

all trains are caught still
no freeways flap close enough to wake us
this night reparations are collected in pores
opened by mutual love for a fifty-first state
free state shape of waning moon or twin bed
state with only room enough for two

AT THE JAPANESE MARKET

tangy seaweed salad
hiccups, sandals, straw mats, sweet egg
eel unraveled
longan like small investments
solitary lunchers
griddle, slurp, clanging plastic udon bowls
the endless noodle the elder will not cut
as if it were a lifeline to her mother's home in Nakasato

ground pearl crème, rice, steaming ginger tea
to trick the skin into an enduring youth
her leg kicking under the table
a nervous condition brought on by her husband's death
left foot tapping to the REM song,
this is the end of the world as we know it
a thin silver hair poking tear duct of her right eye
like salmon bone demanding attention

as a girl she was told this country was the end of the world she knew
she nodded
said nothing
what more was there to understand

mochi stuffed with red bean paste
wooden chopsticks, wasabe in a tube, pickled quail eggs
one thousand silver fish with their eyes intact
video game carjacks
a flutter in her chest
poster for a war movie peeks out from behind the sticker machine
under the bomb a fallen star pear
she squeezes, bruises it,
slides it into her purse before anyone can see

she remembers the weather man telling her today there would be sun
her umbrella knows better
eventually the noodle chases its own tail
the antsy knee will shatter when she falls
the star pear will wither into a heavy coat of loose skin
ever sweet but too worn for market

CANVAS LA

In a room occupied by carpet stains and a short white dog
we sit afflicted by colds brought on by evening runs through sprinklers
Marley's blues bob through air like soothing cough drops
as we practice minute speeches
each one of us a wind-up doll of nuclear facts
for primetime we flyer promos of guerrilla tactics
ask microwave masses to break habits of corruption
we promise there is still time to save this planet, your soul, your dog
there is still strength to stop boulder of apathy
don't let it flatten our dignity
we look deep into stigmatized eyes and say *I trust you*
to deliver your letters of intent to the doorstep of Congress
respectfully require them to uphold humanity
praise their constituents with sweet rains of democracy
tomorrow is growing in your granddaughter's belly
we know you are willing ready able
to open your wallet and make a difference.

CANVAS REDONDO BEACH

nativity on his shingle roof
World Wildlife sticker on his counterpane
Berkeley print stretched across his chest
he answers with jaded breath
what do *you* want
I qualify
I want what *you* want sir
taxes spent on life affirming initiatives
education & health care
not nuclear weapons
protection for...
You murdering bitch!
open door slammed shut
I slam right back
you sir are an extinct beast Berkeley would gladly 86
and Christ, well, he would never bless your rooftop or your front door

FROM THE BACKSIDE OF EL TEMPLO DEL XOL

Teotihuacan, Mexico

tourist don't dare wander behind this sacred prism
where eagles swoop and lizards boast crimson swallows
vendors tired of lowering labor into pesos
bow to avoid eyes of modern day Dons
their arrogance carved with flanked hearts into spine of maguey
names deep as linoleum print of conquest
now pressed into jerseys and sweats
what is left on the backside
are cement sheets painted with blood
segun los guias who use every tactic
to seduce gabacho wide eyes into big tips
above us prayers float in on drunken hummingbirds' wings
sudden and free they parry a millennium of tacit questions
but all I want to know is if we can blend into this ancient compass
make love like serpentine statues
twisted as wild flames on this shadeless day
and get away with a little conquest of our own

ON THE ROAD TO SAN CRISTOBAL
DE LAS CASAS
Chiapas, Mexico

Can you sleep with a semi-automatic in your face?
this is first class baby
reclining seats no chickens the bathroom door stays closed
Terminator I & II on the screen

Where's your passport?
the barrel fits into the canal of your neighbor's ear
four men escorted off like bleating calves
the bus driver continues on

Where's your birth certificate?
in your underwear drawer in your tia's house
in Colonia del Valle about 12 hours north
You are American?
American by birth?
And your VISA?
"I'll be back" the sergeant says and you know
he has seen the movie before

What to do with a pocha on the bus?
What to do with Guatemalans lined up alongside the road?
too many to turn back
too pocha to turn in
a ballpoint pen bribe
nail clippers and a tin of Godavi chocolate
the family will understand
it was me or the truffles
the truffles they say

say goodbye to the Danes
suspected socialists
and the German hippie with only one shoe
the bus driver takes a sip from his flask
what'd I tell ya, this is first class baby

you take a sip too
ask what else there is to watch
something to make us laugh a little

and there from his cabinet he pulls a cassette
of all that is wound right in the world
a Cantiflas video, "Romeo and Juliet"
silly love, man versus his own comic timing

our nerves melt with laughter
abuelos children surviving members of our international load
hyenas in the high mouth of this mountain god

the next stop isn't so bad
even the militia can't help but watch
from the corner of their eyes—a smile
reminder of when Mexico owned Hollywood
la Epoca Dorada, the Golden Age
when a short man with big ears and pouty lips
turned his people to the politics of survival
that is the politics of laughter
contagious as the politics of fear

WOMEN WITH WALK

para las mujeres del Isthmus de Tehuantepec

fast in stride
don't slow down for strays or splinters
earlobes stretched with swaying gypsy lanterns
baskets of jicama on their heads and tissue between breasts
should they have to pee somewhere deep in the Sierra Mixe
they don't wait for sunburnt tourists to begin the bargain race
they take what they ask for nothing less

breaking into rivers
eucalyptus strapped to their back
moon in their belly
a child on each hip
they slip into and out of this isthmus
unaccounted for by any government census

broad and strong
don't waste time on faith
they prefer stone
carved in times when what was   was
they brush their teeth with blood
paint their nails with wings of market flies
as their children steal bread from men
who haven't been home to eat in ten years

stretching our earth's crevices
balanced on torn feet
they spit back sand into sculpture
lungs full of iguana teeth
all the while outlasting famines
feminism and non-profit foundations

BASIC TRAINING

Miguelito writes *Viva Zapata* in dust collected on the van
his fist size of an over-sunned tangerine
in my Bruce Lee camouflage
he tells me I look like *watcho*
watcho?
watcho.

machine gun simulation
of government watchmen
he hides at the river
dares me to jump from a log draped in algae
double dare?
double double dare.

from here you can hear training drills
sharp turns & loading clicks
hand-in-hand
a wasp scares us into action
better to belly flop then be stung
the war paint washes off
his worried look gone young
a smile that says I've completed basic training

BASQUET

a lesson in Tzonzil math

10 fingers of red clay
spread across a midday sun
an impossible shot

14 skirts of black wool
chase and praise each other
ponytails up by one

28 arms for carrying wood and guns
wave for a chance to shoot
love passes love delivers love scores

history is boys waiting
taking their turn on sidelines
eyes fixed on the lassoed god

OLMEC HEADACHE

Jalapa, Mexico

fat face
squint nose
stuck in shadowed showrooms
just begging for a kiss
I see you Father
and I spot you
two thousand years in exchange for this...
that you might grow
Botero wide arms legs and chest
wobble through *their* cities of glass and wire mesh
dig through *their* modern graves
taking from them only the best
with which to start your own museum
now with *their* babies skulls encased
laugh us up an earthquake
and put an end to this nosy race

PALACIO DE BELLAS ARTES
Mexico, D.F.

Inside walls hiccup colors
brighter than Bubble Yum
bursting from Tonantzin's lips
her laughter bouncing off polished tile
as billfold politics call on her to scream
in a million shades of red
this new Mexico is rational!

outside street clowns billow flames
in the shape of plumeless eagles
awing atheists and taxi drivers
in between green lights
face-painted oil barons
mouth with singed lips
this new Mexico is rational

in Maria's Internet Café
arthritic commies sip tea while masked
teenage rebels mass email IMF secretaries
a virus that reads... this new Mexico is rational...
fwd: this new Mexico is rational...

en Estadio Azteca beggars in bleacher stands wave
row by row they cheer on Red Cross nurses
Chicadee boom a la bim boom bah!
Que viva este nuevo Mexico...
Rah! Rah! Rah!

at los Pinos* there are logs
covered with drumlines of devoted termites
served in tacos to children with silver teeth
each with a cleaning uniform that reads
Juan, first son of this new Mexico

in hallowed halls there is comedy
a drunken skeleton of Tin Tan
making love to his left palm on opera night
an endless flicker of florescent light
reveals prayer slips stuck with wads of gum
to the under seat of velvet chairs
dios mio este nuevo mexico es...

in the gift shops there are oxygen masks
and thirty-pound books on Orozco, Siquieros and Rivera
their mistresses chaperoned by robot slaves who flip the pages
an endless stock of postcards advertise
this new Mexico is rational
this new Mexico is rational
stamped and sent out on trails of volcanic smoke
inside swirling ribbons tickle marble slabs
all clean enough to eat on

outside the hunger for edible paint goes on
untamed by the good press

* *los Pinos is the presidential residence in Mexico City*

CHINESE NEW YEAR IN HAVANA

dragons dare drunks to dance on rooftops
lovers twist egg noodles on chop sticks and kiss
between bites bodies drift in with offerings of ron y rice
there is fire in some eyes
distant memories of a land not surrounded by time
long brown legs tight like husked cane
wide hips gripped by callused hands
exiled panthers, pardoned poets and madmen
thumb prints that leave no trace
history burnt off to protect them even here
they share scars and indiscretions
their children tuck fortunes into seashells
passed back-n-forth on the crests of West Indian waves

POLISH

Sancti Spiritu, Cuba

we break into earth one stab at a time
our work song *Sancti Spiritu, Sancti Spiritu*
our harmony careful
we may be sisters but we are still strangers

with the patience of a midwife the ghost of Celia Sanchez watches over us
her fingers long rays of sunshine tilling ageless universal matter

woman here have perfect nails
painted in garnet, corvette, cinnamon red
none chipped, none dirty, perfect-perfect red

all I have are nubs
bitten stumps where my womanhood would be if I'd let it grow
I show my mentor Lourdes my hands and look to where the pigs are slaughtered
she doesn't say a word
which I know from workshops
means there's nothing nice to say

below folds of earthworms are cut in half and I am torn
between letting her know how hungry I am or digging deeper
her laugh unveils my dilemma
taking off her gloves she says, "tienes algo pa'esconder"
nervous because I do have something to hide
even those in solidarity can be a danger to a nation floating outside the box

our last day together
I present her with two new shades
copper/silver—pennies/nickels
loose change planted in the soil of a country
that hasn't forgotten its promise

PORT AU PRINCE

a choir of ebony angels sang on both sides of the plank
leaving thumbprints on my temples
mosquito bites burnt into my sides

as tall as their steel drum
I swayed to its hollow call
wanting to be wielded smooth like that

children sprinted alongside the bus
climbing I wore matching yellow shorts and shirt
a giraffe on the chest and visor with straw bill

some could not stand the guilt
their dollars waving from windows
the barefoot hunger jumping like Go Fish

I did not have to give
but my mother she carried plastic grocery bags
filled with old clothes sandals tennis that no longer fit

the road to El Citadel a wound chambered nautilus
my donkey led by the boy with a gum green watch
that played Chopin's Minute waltz at every quarter hour

when he held my hand to help me down
I knew he knew I loved him
would have held his hand the whole way

but there was a bus to catch, parents watching a five star dinner waiting
a whole nation to attend to
far more hungry than my budding breasts

TRAVEL GUIDES
Verdadero, Cuba

The cock of a modern Master is only hard at dawn and dusk
for twenty minutes a day she congratulates him on his conquest
the rest of their time spent on the balcony of Hotel Paradisus.

Friends from nursing school gather to observe
their respective dates sipping pink drinks by the verandah
off-duty they practice names of body parts in Latin
there is a test next week but one sits quiet
busy with daydreams of pigs bled in her uncle's field
six short corpses drawing nothing but flies.

In the morning she lies still long enough to feel the sweat from his palm
sink into the warm cave between her thighs.
He never knew her name
did not ask her age at dinner
or when she danced for him on jagged parapet of El Morro.

She has been his docent for a week
guided him through the old and new of Havana
translated the menu, taken his pulse, lotioned his back
all to feed her family meat for the month,
buy a bicycle for her brother Leonardo,
who paints naked women on palm fronds—their silhouettes
left to dry in the sun,
and a TV for her oldest Victor
who spends his days cleaning hotel rooms
where he can catch the latest steps broadcast on MTV.

She gossips with her godsister Tita
on local men caught with their pants down
her godsister Tita who has walked this tightrope longer
and can say her alphabet in German, Dutch and Portuguese
her godsister Tita who believes revolution costs nothing
but what you are willing to sell.

GRASS

Squaw Valley, California

I. Sergio pushed the insatiable mower singing Frank Sinatra's
My Way in broken English he did not notice the white moth
caught in swinging blades or his abandoned cigarette
sparking a patch of dry matted grass
with a rubber sole meant to last him three winters he put the cherry out.

II. It took the brothers ten years and 3,500 golf courses
to save enough to bring Doña Lydia here and now that she's home
she sits staring out the window of their single room apartment
dreaming of an uncut green like the one in Lacandon.

III. When you blow on it just right you can set an Andean flute free
postcard of a time when sheep ruled and our only duty
was to play them to sleep with songs of cud and endless campo.

IV. For $5.25 a square foot you can buy a patch of evergreen shag
lady on T.V. says for 59¢ a day you can feed a starving child
I write a check for six and send a letter to my congressman
asking for an increase in home improvement taxes
enough to stretch a football field across the cracked earth of Somalia.

V. Underneath cleats, bent reeds of garden grass are sending out a call to arms
through subterranean telephone wires there is talk of a movement
to take on these overgrown larva with their driving ranges and grazing tanks
to rise up fourteen feet in a day and tame them into lesser beings.

WINDOW SHOPPING ON BROADWAY
Downtown, Los Angeles

she stares at her reflection in the window
a showgirl's figure superimposed
on her own round silhouette
her huipil is stained with red clay
black birds dance across her chest
their caws fending off men
who lean in with *mamacitas* and *bonitas*
their accents and beer steaming the glass

there is no harvest of wool here
no poppy seed dye
crushed red grasshopper
no loom between her legs
here women's feet press cold steel pedals
their sewing machines hidden
behind garage doors here women
dress their worn fingers with band-aids

at the ends of each arm
she sees the palms that once shuttled rainbows
the lines of yarn held tight to the loom
she remembers the rug underbid
by another weaver two stalls down
and her grandmother's plum-stained hands
waving to clot the bleeding sky as her bus pulled out

betrayed by their own uselessness in this new world
her hands press up against the warm glass
beyond her reflection a rack of leopard print
pants suits cut to hug a size six
calling on her to begin the day
in someone else's body

CLEAR GOLD
Imperial Desert, CA

one gallon
two lips
split by a river of endless thirst
hot flood of desert paint
washes off silt semen sweat
and when you arrive
there will be no paradise
just beef jerky
bile and an endless mile to go

a silent rock
balanced on the head of another
a look out cross warped horizon
its every layer touched by the devil's shaking finger
rippling tide of sand
and no man no woman or child
shall be forgotten

five gallons
ten split lips
the thirst of an emptied sea
ravine of shoes and shit and silence
a cactus field of winter roses
shell and somewhere
a young girl carries a water bottle to gym class
an expectant mother fills the dog's bowl
a tired waitress brings her table fifteen cups of ice
lemon margaritas on the rocks
slushies
fountain drinks
courtesy cups
an endless mile to go
twenty-six gallons
fifty-two cracked lips
split with the gush of air

an opened promise
between Rock Mountain and the Arco station on US 2
51 blue flags swarm
desert flies
awkward and bumbling in an alchemist's wind

change is uncertainty of the mind
menace of sanity melting
with each surge on the thermometer
107...108...110 points of lava
walking on hot coals
the endless mile behind you

two water towers sliced
a bloody foot stumbles
between this world and the next
a fever
a succulent plant
a sunrise on stilts
a pair of waning eyes
two cracked lips
a sip of clear gold

RIPE

City of Industry, Los Angeles, CA

sing her a song
a merengue line
a slip on glove
made of lace not plastic

marry her to the fence on Alameda and Manchester
where she stands under parasol of circus colors
cutting symmetrical wedges
coconut cucumber mango mamey

fingers red with chilé
lips a cracked slice of watermelon
tight from salt sticks dipped and sucked on
a desert survival trick

she reads the license plates of each passing car
writes them down in a code no MIT prodigy could break
it is the language of ancestors
glyphs used to transfer an entire civilization to an unknown plane

the clean-up of precious fruit takes ten light changes
two pairs passing in each direction
a steady gutter growl of Broncos and Mactrucks
exhaust of two-ton machinery clinging to her shoulders neck back

in La Ceiba she would make plans for Fridays
be dressed for Club Luna Llena by ten
a DJ and a tent wide enough to set sail for a warless country
her worries dampened with the ardor of good times

today she's too tired to plan such freedoms
the Bandamobile passes Umpa! Umpa! Umpapá!
a reckless toucan blaring
memories of her life before red lights

HE'S GOT THE WHOLE WORLD IN HIS HANDS
San Francisco, CA

black lung flip mop rock breath
swabbing the seams
you see the whole world from here
your own roof in the Mission
the man picking steak from his teeth
the trolley falling back
and Reverend Moss picking his scab in Golden Gate Park

the wind creeps under your hard hat
she whispers *war is on,*
it's an election year,
you'll never know how much they need you
good people of this city
disgusted by your squalid hands
your eternally-black nails
the smell of tar tainting their tranquil day

this morning your daughter
remembered to wash her hands
waiting outside the restroom door
you hold her backpack
cold damp of pipe water
steaming between your palms
as you walked her to class

MERIENDA
Sancti Spiritu, Cuba

women talk over scores of last night's domestic disputes
their nails spread petals of poinsettia
no car no cell phone no house
they own only their loves
wrap themselves tight in them
licking and smoothing the edges like cigar rollers in El Laguito

as we graze on green tomatoes and stale bread
they dissect the latest novela broadcast from Brazil
as they chew and chat
inhale Popular cigarettes
we pick up enough attitude to know the subject is men

city girls we click in similar tongues
how we left our men behind
to travel to school to taste other lips
they laugh, say our men are thick veins in the sides of our necks
throbbing reminders of how weak we can be

what doesn't translate is our pride
an overfed capitalist trademark
the Ego thinking it can do it all, alone
how far we are from love they say
from the surrender, we should be so lucky
to know when not to let go

UN BESO SURREALISTA PARA LAS CINCO
Y PUNTO DE LA TARDE
Madrid, España

Pedro the Cruel has left his jockstrap hanging in the window again.
Cousin Dalí is tanning hides on the rooftop
while Cirque du Soleil cast members play
olley olley oxen free in the garden maze.

North African hustlers slang mix tapes to museum docents
while I sip malt beer to chase down sardines and eggs.

On the way to see the King
I stain *la Güernica* with red lips meant to survive sex
they take me away in a cloisonné egg
to where Señor Lorca is hard at work
digging his own grave on the roadside of this new republic.

What would it be to die for your land your lover your goat?

I chip in, ask what he has planned for the afterlife
he answers, *heaven is making whoopie in the cobalt sands of Atlantis.*
drunk with port stolen from the liquor cabinet of the Queen
we brave the sea, only to drown just out of reach of Asmodea's rock.

CHRISTMAS SHOPPING IN MADRID

slick black leather   strapped to the backs

     of brujas   from Goyas' final days

dark as a moth eyes   they smoke chains around their lungs and mine

timing my move   I dare   to break   their shopping routine

each sucked in face   an excuse   not to give me directions

so who told Columbus   which way   how did the boy

ever find the palace   with all this pushing

and shoving   for gold   did he wander   for days

choking on the people's lack of concern   no wonder

        the man would land so lost

PISCINA PACIFICA

PELIGRO!
NO SWIMMING!
still the three-year-old china poblana goes in
to hide from the water monster
her father, un pelon con seaweed locks
tattooed from his neck to his ankles
with a map of forgotten urban planning districts

a few waves away, surfers, really accounting execs
meditate on spiked hair of Lady Pacific
I have seen her swallow three strong men on a day like this in Manzunte
their boards spit out like toothpicks
from here She's just another calculating club trick
reeling in cholos and cotton swabs alike
her hunger does not differentiate
bones boards bravado
it all goes down the same

oil derricks to my left accent the shit refinery to my right
my mother's voice says it's crude to call it what you want
it's still paradise's bidet
PELIGRO!
my big toe split by a Bud bottle, half full
I want to know why there are dead ladybugs in the sand?
Do islands have feet that tickle the sea floor?
And if high tide is ever ashamed of her lows?

CHILD OF QUESTIONS

"Live your questions now, and perhaps even
without knowing it, you will live along some
distant day into your answers."
—Rainer Maria Rilke

in between the underwear ads and the text of the presidential address
there is the question only a child would dare ask   *why*
in 1941 it cost 5 cents to print the compound equation of all our doubts
six generations later there are still no answers

we appear cleaner than we did yesterday
our hands tied to the remote
we watch shrapnel burrow in an endless desert
an engineering student seared *live!*
the school of mud walls collapses *live!*
a maidservant's lung perched on bayonet *live!*
our perverse uncle burnt in effigy *all live!*

child of questions sing sweet reason
make of your eyes reflecting pools
catch them at their windows
stop them mid-sentence
barking into red phones
their tongues barbed with this nonsensical language
its rules always bending to make way for exclusion
child of questions fight off your ABCs
block print apathy A B U
Abu Haider is taping his windows
he will stand alone to defend his bookstore
his daughter's questions ringing in his head

fifth graders down the hall spin 50 Cent
cause they gonna get rich or die trying
the war drum is bouncing down Hoover in a 67' Impala
red and white stripes whipping from the chrome rims
child of questions driving uninsured
his sagging-jean resolve to get back at The Man
a wardrobe not afforded peace of mind
the terminal *why* scraping cement

TWIN TOWERS
Downtown, Los Angeles

At first glance you look like any other office building
streamlined conveniences; mauve wall, vending machines,
manicured trees

you make it seem easy to enter friendly for visitors
and then at the red light stray eyes stare too long
wondering how any business man or woman
could enjoy a room with no view
slight tease of window a diabetes test strip

if we were to prick your walls with seismic pins
open your slants enough to let light in

how many stones would fall loose? how many elephants would
charge through?

ODE FOR THE MIC

for The World Stage, Leimert Park, LA

through time you stand a shepherd's staff
herding profits and derelicts
heroes too
souls intent to do right by the world
under red light
spit in your pores
an obelisk dipped in honey
you stand to make love
like stela in Copan
resurrecting history with each voice

I've seen men catch seizures after just one dance
hurling through their concrete façade
I've seen you make them cry
still they come back
with whooping cough confessionals
in solemn whispers
in eloquent rage
the pay off is hearing their name called

you are Pied Piper's flute
Trinity's anchor
Moari spear
Jacobin's bayonet
San Andreas faultline trembling
Liberty's backbone aching
thermometer rising
bass string pulled tight
playing the scales of our breathing
our over-heating
our melancholy brand of new world jazz
an antenna calling all channels home
and when the city burns again
you'll prove descendant of Black Eye Brahma
digging center to where sanctuary waits

and when the bombs drop too close
you'll turn pole vault
lifting us over and out of despair

and when they finally discover the dissidents
planning revolt in your lair
you'll turn Katana blade

til death you'll stand
and should that day come
we, the poets, will have our own Iwojima
raise you from the soft skin of death
to your rightful post center stage   all eyes on you

THE DAY I HUGGED SONIA

for Sonia Sanchez

a thousand bobby pins
jumped from the island virgin's hair
as she read of white petals and cosmic touch
heart to lung
a chorus of katydids sung
with Sonia suddenly the Muse seemed noble and fair

the day I hugged Sonia
the streets of South Central held an impromptu parade
in her honor children spun ribbons around streetlights
maypoles and madrigals
there was dizzy joy
bubbling up from the shanties of Santo Domingo
and in Quahiniqualapa black was beautiful again

the day I hugged Sonia
atheists took to forgotten maps in the stars
only to find their families waiting
at Union Station beggars were anointed
with Frankensence and Myrrh
the Earth shook along its laugh lines
and the pen in the hand of the White House
could not hold still long enough to sign off on war

the day I hugged Sonia
a monsoon of good will struck my right cheek
and being reborn I could not fight back
a window opened in my chest
a feverish pot of rice and peas thrown out
a desperate need to feed the world
to scratch and pull at the scalp of freedom
until it tingled with possibilities
and it would be naïve to think
she felt such things in my humble embrace
but she would have had to been blind

to not see the smile on God's face
when Sadako's paper cranes turned flesh and feather
lifting cataracts of smog from the pupils of our estranged cities
able to see for the first time
people gathered in parking lots to dance under an ultramarine sky

the day I hugged Sonia
a life time of poetry didn't seem so long
didn't seem long enough

INDIA

for the children of Shaw, NE, D.C.

you were seven
the world ancient
everyday you took the globe home in your backpack
as if it were a basketball or bundt cake
you took it out to show others
this is where we are — right here
that spot is home

the day the tanks came to 6th & S
you wanted to welcome the men on duty
"they're here to help," you said and took them sweet bread
while we, the grown folk, stood behind the gates of fear and contempt
they smiled at you, dropped their aim to the floor
you took out the globe
showed them the spot
you told them they were home
and for that moment they were

that summer our block was red, white and blue
with blood and flood lights
police cars and sergeants
the war was fought while we ducked under tables
16 deaths under the age of 21
you made cards for the mothers
with a picture of the world and a star
lingering above the words "this is home"

I knew then you were not of this Earth
still I clung to your geography
you made it seem the world wasn't so heavy
and with enough sugar you could change
the aim and intentions of men
you were seven
the war ancient
still you carried us all
in your backpack they found crumbs and a compass
directions home should we be lost without you

IN THE MASTER'S YARD
October 16, 1995

We hang like voodoo dolls above the masses
only today there are no nooses
it is before Islam is a flaming pitch fork in Grant Wood's hand
before we land on Mars
before even dust.

Maya Angelou is rising from pulpit
a floating soulful Buddha
first lady of healing
her minister of music, Stevie, can't see the masses
but he knows them by the smell of sandalwood and sweat
one man for each hair standing on his back

today the scars of the whip
heal with balm of brotherly love
oils and incense burn
today, you say "Al salaam a'alaykum"
like you've been saying it all your life
like you mean it
cause you do

from the trees we descend
mixed hued girls with no roots
there's no one to tell us to go home
and if they did we wouldn't know which way to run
lost in a mist of vendors
marking the date with commerative plates and pens
tomorrow the news will say 50,000
but proof is in your pictures
shots of rolling waves
under a perfect mesh of cloud and light
framing a million promises made this day

man to man
man to woman
man to mirror
it is before you become mother to an endangered species

before my godson will learn the burden and blessing of his brown skin
before hunters have had their fun with him
Mr. Farrakhan approaches the mic with his swagger step
and though no man is perfect
you can see if the possibility exists it is here
in the smile of the son on his father's shoulders
listening as if his life depended on it
cause maybe it does

it is before I throw your bad choices in your face
and you say, my problem is I thin my poems
make me immune to my own vices
like the drug dealer I've imported from back home
who has cone to be made "man" among men
he looks lost, bronze faced with sun-bleached dreads
Malcolm T-shirt on and Africa medallion
Unity bandanna and cowry shell ring
he has converted
he is sorry
and tonight will bed down
with no thought to the clients
feigning for him to come home

forgiveness is a prayer mat at the Capitol exit
an underground railroad
and all are free to get off
stroll past Master's house
picnic on his front lawn
Salat and sunset
lawyer, mailman, preacher, beggar
of humanity let them say this
there was a day when hate was chased from the Hill
fearing the free would riot and tear the hallowed halls down
and when there was only prayer and hope to accuse them of
the masses stood guilty of believing change would come

BOTTOM OF THE NINTH

There are no pedestrian crossing signs in Tikrit

red eye target running so low

Lt. Gomez shot

and if war were turned inside out

if it was your life or theirs wouldn't you have done the same

                                        a boy running

                                        towards home

towards goat herd

a tin roof haven

a good man would have aimed lower

soldier, today you are God

let no child be left behind

the few. the proud. the brave.

dressing wounds

cameraman watching

12 billion eyes are on you

Lt. Gomez shot to protect his patrol

and if it was your life or theirs wouldn't you have done the same

(this material may not be suitable for children under the age of 12)

still, the eyes of the world can not look away

a 40 inch flat screen at the Burbank airport

suits sip Stoli, Heineken draft

diet Pepsi and pizza lodged in their molars

"Put the Dodger game on!"

today Lima is God

a shutout

the boy stuck between bases and a small tin haven

a field of goats

child with one run to go

his father's walls face west   he did not see his son fall

the sand in Lt. Gomez' socks

a pillar of regret on the chopper floor

Lt. Gomez declined to speak to the cameras

bottom of the ninth

all bases loaded

Lt. Gomez cradles the boys head

a last breath

a last hit   a foul ball

but who's keeping score

"I learned about life
from life itself,
love I learned in a single kiss
and could teach no one anything
except that I have lived
with something in common among men,
when fighting with them,
when saying all their say in my song."

From "Ode to the book"
Pablo Neruda